A Kids Guide To Owning A Spaniel

Tabitha and Matilda Jacob

Assisted by

Anne-Marie Millard

Copyright © 2015 Tabitha and Matilda Jacob

All rights reserved.

ISBN: 151182784X
ISBN-13: 978-1511827843

DEDICATION

None of us at Uggeshall Kennels could work without the quiet never-complaining presence of Matilda and Tabitha's Maternal Grandmother 'Mille'. Known far and wide by all as 'MorMor' (Danish for Mothers Mother), Mille is always on hand to help, armed with a mop and bucket or a much needed cake, we all want to say a huge thank you to her for just being so wonderful.

CONTENTS

Acknowledgments

1   A Little Bit About Spaniels

2   Meeting Your Puppy

3   Choosing A Name

4   What You Need To Buy

5   Getting Your House ready

6   Living With Your Puppy

7   Grooming

8   Name Games

9   Walking

10   Sit, Stay and Drop

11   Socializing Your Puppy

12   Doggy Days

13   Remember

ACKNOWLEDGMENTS

I would like to say a big thank you to my year three teacher at Reydon Primary School, Mr Patterson. He has been the best teacher I have ever had, he makes lessons really interesting and is always there to encourage and support me and my friends.

Matilda

My friends Charlie and Cassidy at Beccles Free School are always there for me, when I am finding things difficult or just need cheering up, so I would like to say a big thank you to them both.

Tabitha

And last, but very much not least, all the generous people that let us use their photos (in random order) :-

Nanette Hall, Gary Broughton and Ollie, Jacqui Cornock and Samuel, Teresa Read, Julian Hammond and family, Andrea, Angela Last, Ceri Browes, Darren Jordan, Donna Spark, Emma o Kelly, Hayley Lockwood, Karen Wilson, Kelly Taylor, Lucy Gilkes, Nicki Gosling, Sheila Peskitt and Rory Peskitt, Sally Dodd, Zac and Luna, Jackie, Nigel, Rosie and Dixie.

Tabitha & Matilda

INTRODUCTION

Our names are Tabitha and Matilda Jacob and we live in North Suffolk in England. Our family owns and runs a kennels where we breed dogs. The type of dogs we breed are 'Spaniels'. We also have a 'small-holding' where we have goats, sheep, ducks, chickens, cats and ponies. So we have a lot of animals to deal with every day.

We breed three different types of Spaniels – Springer Spaniels, Cocker Spaniels and Sprocker Spaniels. We both have our own dogs that we help look after. As we have got older we have been given more and more responsibility with our own dogs. Tabithas's dog is called 'Jade', she is a black female Cocker spaniel. Matilda's dog is called 'Blue' and she is a liver and white Springer spaniel.

Mum asks us to help with the puppies we are going to sell. Sometimes we play and look after the pups for fun, sometimes we work with the puppies for pocket money.

We have both learnt an awful lot of stuff about Spaniels and we would like to share it with you.

1 A LITTLE BIT ABOUT SPANIELS

Spaniels can be your best friend. You can tell secrets to them and they will never woof a word to anyone. They can give you the best cuddles in the world (nearly as good as your parents), Spaniels make you happy, and come and find you when you are sad. They like splashing in puddles, running through fields and cuddling up with you in front of the television.

BUT having your own Spaniel is not all fun and games. There is a lot of hard work to be done and, if the puppy is going to be a family puppy, then you need to do some of the work too. Some of the work is fun, some of the work might be a bit boring but it will be worth it in the end.

Let's begin by looking at the different types of Spaniel we breed, love and look after.

English Springer Spaniels

These are the first spaniels we owned. Some people think they are a bit nutty, but they are not! Springers come in two different colours. They can be black and white or they can be liver (brown) and white. Sometimes you can have a Springer which is three colours (brown, black and white) but these can be hard to find.

They do come in different shapes and sizes. We find the bigger Springers (like 'Blue') are a bit quieter and the smaller Springers (like 'Sky') are a bit more excitable. Both make perfect pets. They are very good at doing what they are told, and they learn things very quickly.

Cocker Spaniels

Cockers are a little bit smaller than the Springers and are quite different in character.

The girl Cocker spaniels like a lot of attention and can sometimes be a bit naughty and ignore what you are saying to them. But they love their owners and like to try and sit on their owner's laps and give them huge cuddles if they are allowed. Boy Cockers are great fun and like to run off with your shoes, homework or television remote controls. Parents sometimes do not find this funny but we do!

Cockers can come in many different colours: Ours are golden, brown, black, fox-red, and lemon (pale yellow). You can also get ones which are two colours like the

Springers.

Sprocker Spaniels

Sprockers are a cross between Springers and Cockers. This means the Mother is a Springer and the Dad a Cocker (or sometimes the other way round).

Sprockers are in between Springers and Cockers in size and can be black, brown, gold, black and white and brown and white. They are very nosy and like to know what is going on. If you are doing your homework they like to sit on your feet. If you go and look in the fridge then they like to try and actually get in the fridge to have a closer look. They can be naughty but they can also be very good.

All the different types of Spaniels make great family pets but, like us, they all have very individual good bits and bad bits so it's best to let an adult talk to the breeder to find out which is the best Spaniel for you.

2 MEETING YOUR PUPPY

We are lucky enough to sometimes see the pups being born but we are not allowed to touch and must keep quiet so we don't upset the Mum whilst she is having her pups. When puppies are born, they can't see yet but can still make a noise. We sometimes wake up in the night and hear the new pups squeaking away in the room next to us.

The puppies eyes don't start to work until they are 2 to 3 weeks old. This means that they are very sensitive to noise from the big wide world. They also use their sense of smell so they can wiggle their way to their Mother's milk.

When the puppies are a few weeks old they can start to walk but they still cannot see very well. So it is very important that we don't scare the puppies with loud voices and crashing and banging around.

Some Spaniel Mothers will be very pleased to show off her new babies to people, some will be very worried about strangers coming to have a look so it is important to be thoughtful about how  you act in front of the Mother and the pups. Being crowded by noisy people, especially high pitched kids, can be very distressing for both Mum and pups. So you need to be extra quiet and considerate if you get the chance to see both Mum and pups together.

When the pups are a bit older, breeders normally let the Mother dog have a break while people visit to choose their new puppy. This still means though you need to be very grown up and sensible. The puppy's view us as giants and the noise we normally make (and we are quite LOUD) is very loud to them and is also very scary.

So you need to be quiet, and listen to what you are being asked to do. However if you have read this book then you can just impress the breeder by being the most well-mannered kids ever!

Not only do pups see us as noisy giants, we also have very big feet. So, just to make sure you don't hurt anything, your best bet is to sit down and keep your feet still. If you would like to hold the pup then you need to ask politely and ask if you can sit on the floor with the puppies.

Depending on the age of the pups, some will run over to you, some will stay back and try and suss you out. The safest way to hold a pup is to sit on the floor with your legs straight out in front of you  and have the pup placed on your lap. You can then gently hold the pup in place on your lap and say hello. If you suddenly get worried you are going to let the pup slip, then don't be shy, and just ask for some help. That will show how grown up you are. If you need to then get up off the floor, then do it slowly taking care not to kick you giant feet out and scaring or hurting anyone. If you do all that, then you are going to be a great puppy owner.

Pups love nibbling at things, at this point in their lives they are using their mouths just like we use our hands, exploring all these new shapes, sizes and smells. So please expect that you might get nibbled. They won't hurt you, but sometimes their baby 'pin' teeth can get caught on clothes, shoe laces and they all love nibbling kids with long hair (Matilda has had a LOT of experience with this) so if you have longer hair then your best bet is to tie it back.

Puppies don't like:

- Rapid PAT PAT PAT
- Holding on too tight or squeezing
- Being picked up quickly
- Being grabbed

Puppies like:

- Gentle slow strokes
- Touching without grabbing
- Being careful around ears and eyes

For the first few weeks of their lives puppies are just fed milk by their Mums. This can make a rather funny smell when they poo and wee it out. So don't be shocked if the place they are in doesn't smell quite right. You are just not used to pup smells, we don't even notice it now.

Choosing your puppy can be difficult – some breeders of pups choose for you. That makes it a lot easier since they know all about you and your family AND they know all about their own dogs. However if you are to choose your own pup then you need to have decided if you want a boy or a girl, what sort of colour you like and what sort of nature it should have. Some people like quiet shy puppies, some like bouncy ones. You also need to remember that the pup won't stay small forever, so you need to have had a look at what size the grown up version of the puppy will be and make sure you like the look of it.

Don't expect to take the puppy home the day you meet it. Most pups stay with their Mums and breeders for at least eight to nine weeks. And it is very important that they do. Taking it any earlier is cruel to both puppy and Mother since they need their mums milk and special care for the first couple of months of their lives.

You can leave the puppy safe with its Mum and you need to go home and get planning and shopping!

3 CHOOSING A NAME

Picking a name that the whole family likes can be very difficult. Some families argue amongst themselves and come up with a list of possible names, some families that come to us, choose one person to pick the name – that is usually the easiest way but not everyone thinks that is fair.

You need to remember that the name you pick will be around for a long time. So if you decide you like the name 'Princess Bubblegum' or 'Doctor Who' when you are quite little, how are you going to feel about that name when you are a teenager?

You need to be happy (as does the rest of the family) in calling the name out in public. When you are a teenager calling 'Princess Bubblegum' out across the local park might make you feel pretty silly.

A name that rhymes with something a bit rude is not a good idea either….

Just as your parents put a lot of thought into your name, then you have to put the same special thought into your puppy's name too.

Some puppies come with posh 'kennel names' (but not all) – these are the names the breeder has chosen for the pup but they are not names you use yourself.

For example our lovely Teddy is called 'Gunsmoke Gold Finch', and our Ruby 'Uggeshall Ruby Dragon'. 'Uggeshall' is our kennel name, so that shows that we bred Ruby from two of our own dogs. Our Mother chooses the posh kennel names, we are not allowed to since she apparently really enjoys doing it.

Here are some ideas for you to get started with. Names can be broken down into different groups:

Female names:-

Tilly, Sadie, Gracie, Elly, Esme, Ava, Dolly, Elsa, Pippa, Phoebe, Cora, Thea

Boys names:-

Milo, Ben, Billy, Barney, Ted, Bernie, Finn, Monty, Archie, Otis, Bobby, Harry

Flowers:-

Daisy, Violet, Lily, Rosie, Blossom, Lilac

Sweet stuff:-

Rolo, Cookie, Orea, Fudge, Biscuit, Caramel, Smartie, Buttons, Peanut, Humbug, Polo, Kipling

Funny names:-

Bilbo, Snowball, Hobbit, Pluto, Pugsley, Diva

Some people find it helpful to write a short list of names they like down and then go and see the puppy again.

4 WHAT YOU NEED TO BUY

There are a few very sensible things you need to buy and there are lots of fun things you can buy. But you do not really need a lot of toys – pups can only play with one thing at a time!

Collar and Lead

Buy a collar that can be made bigger. They usually have sizes written on them so you need to point parents to the collars marked 'Size 1 -2'. This means the collar will be small enough to fit the pup when you take them home, but can also be made bigger as the puppy grows. Please remember to check that (as your pup grows) the collar is not too tight.

The best collar and leads to begin with are made of 'nylon' and come in lots of colours and patterns. You will need a little training lead to begin with and then you can move up to a longer and thicker lead.

You will also need a name tag on your dog's collar with your name and telephone number on just in case they get lost.

Beds, Crates and Blankets

A puppy's first bed needs to be one that easily fits into a washing machine – they do get them very dirty! Ones that look snuggly and are machine washable are the best.

Crates are safe places for your dog to have their bed. They are great for going in the boot of the car so the pup (and dog) are safe and don't jump over seats and become dangerous. You can use a crate to make your pup a den in a safe part of the house. You need to think about how big the puppy is going to grow to and  buy a crate big enough for your fully grown dog. The breeder will tell you what size you need.

A puppy blanket can be left with your puppy and his Mother, so when you bring the puppy home to your house he has something comforting to remind him of his mums smell.

Food and Bowls

Firstly you need to find out what food the breeder is feeding  your puppy on so you can buy the exact same one. If you give your puppy a different type of food than that he is used to, he will get a very upset tummy that you will have to clear up.

You will need food and water bowls – these come in many shapes and sizes but it is best to get ones that are 'non-slip' so they don't go sliding across your kitchen floor.

Toys

There are lots and lots of different toys you can buy for a puppy. We always use just three types – a kong that they can chew, a kong wubba they can run around with and a soft toy they can play and sleep with.

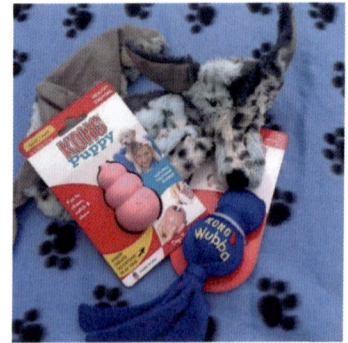

Grooming Kit

You will need a double sided brush and some mild shampoo.

Puppy Pads

If you are not going to use old newspapers to house train your puppy, you can buy puppy pads which look like unfolded nappies…

5 GETTING YOUR HOUSE READY

As you now know, puppies love exploring their world with their mouths; chewing, nibbling or trying to eat stuff so it is very important that there is nothing dangerous for them to chew on in your home. Let the grown ups sort out anything electrical, your job is down on your hands and knees.

Being smaller than an adult, you have a better viewpoint of all the places a pup could want to explore. Puppies love getting wedged behind things and your job is to pretend you are a pup and look for all the places you might want to get stuck in. Behind the fridge? That's always a good one. Beside the oven? Sticky and dangerous at the same time.

How easy are you kitchen cupboards to open? Billy the Springer can open any cupboard door with his nose and likes to have a very good look inside them in case something tasty is hidden in there. It might be a good idea to put child locks on them, not for you but for your puppy of course!

Get yourself a pen and notebook and investigate each room at a time writing down everything as you go.

The garden is also a great place of adventure to a puppy. So it is a hands and knees job here too. You don't want your puppy escaping into the big wide world, so look for holes and escape routes under your fences. These will need to be blocked up even if they are really small, pups are good at wiggling under things.

Some plants and flowers are poisonous to dogs and pups but this is an adult job – just make sure they do it!!

Once all this is done it is time for a family meeting. Rules have to be agreed by everyone otherwise they won't stay rules for very long. A chart of who is responsible for what needs to be drawn up.

Here are the most important rules which need to be decided:

- Is the puppy allowed upstairs?
- Is the puppy allowed in the bedrooms?
- What rooms is the puppy allowed in?
- Where is the puppy going to sleep?
- Who is going to feed the pup?
- Who is going to clean up after pup?

Here is one of our charts:

Puppy jobs – weekend

Activity	Name	Done
Let Out For Morning Wee	Tabby	√
Feed Breakfast	Tabby	√
Take Outside For A Walk	Tilly	√
Clean Up Poo	Mum	√
Training Walk	Tabby	
Feed Lunch	Tilly	
Take Outside After Lunch	Tilly	
Clean Puppy Bed / Crate	Mum	
Feed Dinner	Tabby	
Final Play	Tilly & Tabby	

We have different charts for school holidays, weekends and school days. We work it around what we (as the kids) can do alongside our school work. As we have got older we have taken on more responsible jobs. When people come here to meet our dogs, Tabitha will always be expected to being look after Jade, and talk to the families about her dog.

We are also responsible (now we are older) for our own belongings. So we must not leave any temptation in the way of any possibly naughty puppies. Lego and Play-do was always Billy the Springer's favorite toy to eat, as was Barbie dolls and Action Men. Billy was a very naughty puppy!!!

Finally you need to decide where the puppy is going to call home – his own "bedroom" if you like. This must be a very safe area, with nothing dangerous to chew on, and a place he cannot escape from. He needs to have his bed (possibly in his crate), his water bowl and some newspapers or puppy pads for 'accidents'.

When you have done all this – you should be nearly ready to pick the puppy up and bring him to his new home.

6 LIVING WITH YOUR PUPPY

The first few days with your new puppy are very important. The days need to be calm, not too noisy and you need to concentrate on setting out a good routine for you and your pup.

However excited you are it is probably better just to let your parents pick the puppy up from the breeders. They will have some questions they still want to ask and it is important that the puppy has a calm, quiet journey to his new house.

The moment your puppy gets home he needs to be shown when his bathroom is going to be. So you can take him into the garden and let him have a sniff round 'his' area and hopefully he will go to the loo. Then you need to give lots of praise and take him indoors.

Now you can proudly show him his new 'bedroom' complete with smelly blanket from his mum and some new toys. However much you would like to play with him, the best thing to do is to leave him alone for a bit and let him explore him new space.

He will probably start to make a bit of a fuss, but try to ignore him and go and do something else. After a while you can let him out, and your goal for the day is to keep him awake and entertained in a calm way so at bed time he will hopefully be so tired he will just go to sleep (and not cry for his brothers and sisters).

You can make a start on your responsibility chart straight away.

Feeding:

His first meal at home is important. Fill up the bowl with the right amount of food. Our mum normally gives us a mug or cup which will hold the right amount of food for each meal.

Before you put the bowl down, let him sniff the dish and lick a bit from your fingers so he knows you are in charge.

You can try and make him 'sit' now. While he is standing in front of you, move your hand over his eye line and say 'sit'. Most pups do tend to sit down just so they can then see into your eyes.

Then place the bowl in front of the pup and let him eat. If he leaves some then just take the bowl away. Make sure there is lots of fresh water near the puppy so he can have a drink after he has eaten.

Now is an important time. Take the puppy outside and just let him wander around. You want him to be going to the loo and not getting too distracted by you playing with him. When he finally goes lots of praise – not too much though, you save the BIG praise for when he 'sits' or 'stays'.

7 GROOMING

You need your puppy getting used to being bathed and brushed as soon as possible. When they are very little you can wash them in the kitchen sink, and when bigger, in a bath. BUT they are very slippery when wet so it is best to get an adult to help – you don't want the puppy to slip out your hands onto the floor.

Be prepared to get wet. Have everything ready: shampoo, towels, jug and the water run in the bath or sink. You want the water to be warm, so you can put your hand in it easily. Put the puppy in gently and hold on to the collar. Pour the water with the jug all over the pup and then put some shampoo on. Bubble this up and then wash it off using the jug again. Then quickly out onto a bath mat and then cover the pup with the towel and give them a good dry. Don't let go to early otherwise the puppy will shake and you will get very wet!!

Brushing and grooming is easy. You just need to be gentle and start by doing a little bit at a time. Some pups love it and some hate it. A soft brush all over their body once a day is all you need to begin with.

8 NAME GAMES

Puppies are very quick at learning their names and it's a good game you can play about the house when he first arrives.

Start off in a small room letting your pup scamper about. You sit on the floor but don't encourage the puppy to come to you, just sit quietly and let him play. When he is a small distance  away from you, call his name and get his attention by clapping your hands together. When he comes to you, give him lots of praise (you can give him a treat if you want) and then let him go off and play again. Do this five or six times, no more, you don't want him getting bored of the game too quickly.

You can slowly work up to bigger spaces and as you both get better at it you can try standing up and calling his name. He might not be able to see your face so bend down with your arms outstretched and call him from there.

Once he comes all the time you can start hiding around

the house. You might have to call his name a few times but he will soon get the hang of finding you!

Before you let him off his lead in the big wide world you want to feel confident that he knows his name and he knows you as his owner so you can practice this in the garden to as much as you like. Try a short distance first and then you can work up to hiding in the garden too.

9 WALKING

A puppy should have no more than five minutes a day per month of age; so a three month old puppy would have five minutes x three equaling 15 minutes of walking. You can do this twice a day.

The first job you can do in the garden. This is getting your puppy used to a lead. Attach a 'training' lead (which is a very light and short lead) and let your puppy trail it about for a bit with you watching him at all times so he doesn't get the lead caught around anything and really hurt himself.

We normally sit on the grass and watch. After a while we call the pup to us (giving lots of praise when he comes) and then gently take hold of the lead. At first he will bounce around pulling on the lead, but you keep holding on. Call him to you again, and when he comes (and the lead goes loose) then lots of praise. Do this for about five minutes every day to begin with.

When the puppy seems to be used to the idea of the lead then you can try your first walk. You are not going to get very far! You are going to need to be patient and give him lots of reassurance. Some puppies bounce all over the place. Some pups just lie down and refuse to move.

Try to walk the pup between a wall, a fence or a line of trees so you have a corridor for the pup to walk down. Keep the lead short and upright and gently persuade the puppy that walking beside you is the safe thing to do.

Try not to let the puppy pull. So every time the puppy pulls away from you, you stop. When you stop the puppy will turn to see why he can't move anymore, which makes the lead loose. At this point you praise him and then carry on walking as long as the lead stays loose. This is going to take a long while but it will work in the end.

10 SIT, STAY AND DROP

Teaching your puppy to sit is important. Not only can you use it if you think he is going to jump all over friends, but it is very good in an emergency if you need your pup to stop RIGHT NOW....front door left open? Homework falling off the table? Piece of chocolate dropped on the floor? Saying 'sit' becomes important.

There are two ways you can teach 'sit'. The first one is just with your open hand. Stand in front of the puppy and just put your hand over his eye line. The pup should naturally sit back so they can see you directly.

The second one is to hold a treat in your hand (keep your hand gently closed). Holding your hand at the pups nose level so he can smell the treat, slowly move your hand towards him, up and slightly over his head. As he watches the treat, he'll fold his hind legs under and sit down. Say the word 'sit', lots of praise and then give him the treat.

If you find your pup is moving away, try working in a

corner, this will limit the amount of room he has to move about.

Once you have mastered the sit command you can move on to 'stay'. The first few times you want to ask your puppy to sit and wait a moment before you praise and give him a treat.

Then you can move up to counting in your head. So say 'sit', count to five slowly in your head and then give him the treat. Do this lots and lots until your puppy sits still and doesn't move at all whilst waiting for his treat.

You can now start saying 'sit' followed by 'stay'. Count to ten in your head and give him the treat. Now you need to start making it harder for him. Say 'sit-stay' and then walk a couple of steps backwards.

Once you have your pup just sitting and staying all the time whilst you slowly move away you make it harder by making your pup sit and stay whilst you do something else like put your toys away or help Mum wash up.

If the pup starts ignoring you and trying to wander off, go back to the beginning with just the basic 'sit' command and start again.

Don't worry though, once you and your pup have mastered the sit and stay commands you will feel really pleased with yourself. It might take a long time, but it is worth it.

The final important command to learn is 'drop'. Our

pups love running off with socks so we teach the word 'drop' as soon as we can!

Start with a long toy or their favorite blanket. Take hold of one end as your puppy holds the other in his mouth. Show him the treat in your other hand and then say 'drop'. When he lets go of the toy or blanket, immediately give him the treat.

Now do it again – you want your puppy to think of this as a game. When he becomes good at this, try a different toy. Do not chase the pup though if he decides to scamper off with it, just show him the treat and tell him to drop.

You need to practice this a lot – it is very important you do not chase though. You don't want the puppy thinking that running off with things and you chasing him is a fun game.

Puppies love to chew (as do grown up dogs too). Your job is to teach him what he can chew and what he is not allowed to chew. This is when the 'drop' command becomes very important.

Buy a few hollow hard rubber toys that you can stuff with things to chew. To begin with you can just put in a few of his biscuits, these will be easy for your pup to get. As he gets better at the new game, then you start making it a bit more challenging by adding stuff like dog treats or applesauce and then freeze the toys. This will keep them busy with a frozen snack to enjoy.

11 SOCIALIZING YOUR PUPPY

Once your pup is used to being on a lead then you need to start showing them the big wide world. Our mum brings the puppies (and the older dogs too sometimes) to school to pick us up. She puts the puppies in a crate in the back of the car and then parks near the school gates. She opens the boot, so the puppies can look out and watch us all come out of school. This gets them used to lots of new things; other kids, noise, cars and the school bus. When the pups are older mum brings them up to the gates on a lead so they meet lots of new people and other dogs too.

You need to show your puppy as many things as possible – policemen, firemen, lollipop ladies, other dogs on lead, horses, motorbikes and anything else you can think of. Puppies need to learn that people come in all shapes and sizes, that things like prams, scooters, bikes, wheelchairs, people on skates or crutches are just as safe and fun as you are.

A puppy that has had lots of socializing will something new and think 'oh good – someone new who I can say hello to', ones that have not had lots of socializing will think 'MONSTER!' and then try to get away or bark at them.

Even things around your home – things you think of as normal – can scare a little pup. So as early as you can you need your puppy to be used to things like the vacuum cleaner or the washing machine.

Remember – you are there to make your puppy feel safe so you need to be there and reassure him just like your parents would you.

Bringing your friends round after school needs to be given some thought. Not everyone likes dogs, and quite a few kids (and adults) are scared of them. So if your friends are worried about meeting your pup then you can do one of two things. Firstly you can put your puppy away in a safe room (his bedroom for example) and they don't have to meet him at all. Even some of our friends are very scared of dogs, so we just put the big dogs away in a safe room or a kennel.

If your friends would like to meet the puppy that's good, but it is best to put the puppy in his crate if your friends are a little scared. They can then say hello to each other through the crate itself.

Some of your friends are going to be very excited about meeting your new pup – you have probably told them all about him. But it is much better if it is one friend at a time, too many kids around a pup is very scary for him. Just let them play with him for 10 – 15 minutes and then say it's time for your pup to have a rest and just pop him back in his crate.

12 DOGGIE DAYS

Your pup will not stay small forever and will grow into being one of your best friends. There are lots of things you can go out and do with your dog that both of you will love and turn you into the ultimate team.

Agility:

This is open to any dogs but spaniels are great at it. You can practice at home by making your own agility course, or you can join a club with other dog owners. It even comes a competitive sport, being a timed race on how quickly (and efficiently) you go round the course. Seconds are taken off your time for every obstacle you might knock down or not do properly).

Dog shows:

There are lots of local dog shows where you can take your dog. There will be competitions for the best trained dog, the prettiest eyes or even the waggiest tail.

Dog training classes:

You might want to start doing one of these when your puppy is still young. It is a great way for your pup to meet other puppies and people and for you to have some support with your training. The Kennel Club run a scheme called 'The good citizen dog scheme' where you can be taught how to make your dog a model citizen and a perfect member of your family.

Flyball:

If your dog loves running after tennis balls then this is the perfect sport for you both. Your dog has to learn how to jump over hurdles whilst racing towards a spring loaded box that contains a tennis ball. He will release the ball, and race back to you – it's very fast!

Of course you don't need or want to do any of the above, just spending time walking and playing with your spaniel will make them very happy.

It is going to take you a long while to train your puppy but it will be very worth it in the end – take our word for it!

13 REMEMBER

Having a puppy of your own is a great time for you, but you need to remember that your spaniel is looking for a best friend too, and someone who is going to look after them in this new big bright world.

If you do a good job now and get things right, you will always have a best friend in your dog; no matter how good or bad your day has been either at school or at home, whether you have been told off or just need a cuddle, your puppy will always be there for YOU!

ABOUT THE AUTHORS

Matilda and Tabitha live with their family at Uggeshall Kennels in North Suffolk. Living, breeding, and looking after dogs and puppies is part of their daily life, Matilda is more keen on baking the dog treats and playing with the puppies whilst Tabitha is in charge of junior puppy training. In the past they have found themselves insides dog crates keeping young pups company, Tabitha has helped 'wheel chair' train one of their fine Cocker pups 'Pluto' and they both spend a lot of time helping socialise each new litter both with themselves, their friends and any other occupants of their small holding land. They are both on hand on busy days, meeting and greeting potential owners and helping say good bye to their fledging pups on other days.

Ably assisted by their Mother - Anne-Marie Millard - who runs the kennels alongside her partner Richard Botwright. Anne-Marie has been a writer and a freelance journalist in a more glamorous past. Nowadays will find her, Richard, Matilda and Tabitha usually happily surrounded by Spaniels.